ROLLER COASTERS
PHOTOS + FACTS

016

A BRIGHTLY PHOTO-FACT BOOK

Copyright @ 2023, Brightly Books
2nd Edition, 2024, Brightly Books

All rights reserved. This book or any portion thereof may not be reproduced or used in any manner whatsoever without the express written permission of the copyright holder.

www.brightlybooks.com

Roller coasters are exciting rides, usually found in theme parks.

They zoom around on tracks that go up, down, and all around— even upside down!

People wait in long lines to ride these amazing attractions!

Roller coasters don't have engines— they're powered by gravity.

A roller coaster's cars are pulled up a big hill at the start of the ride.

Once a roller coaster starts moving, it likes to keep moving.

Brakes on the track grip the cars and help the roller coaster slow down.

Riding a roller coaster can be a little scary.

But ride engineers make sure roller coasters are fun *and* safe.

Building a roller coaster takes a lot of work.

Every part must be strong and secure.

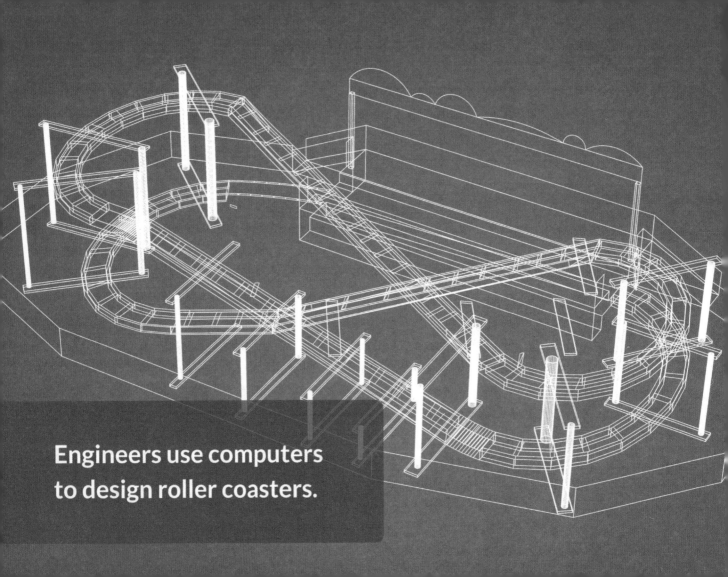
Engineers use computers to design roller coasters.

They plan carefully to make sure rides are exciting, not dangerous.

There are many different kinds of roller coasters.

Each type of roller coaster offers a different kind of thrill.

Wooden roller coasters are often older and can be a bit bumpy.

Steel roller coasters are smoother and can do loops and twists.

Inverted roller coasters have seats that hang under the track.

The riders' feet dangle in the air!

Hypercoasters are really big and really fast— almost as fast as a race car!

Roller coasters can have cool themes, like pirates or space travel.

Roller coasters are so cool!

Printed in Great Britain
by Amazon